AF422536

My communication book

Get to know me!

My name is_______________________________________

My friends call me_________________________________

My favorite color is_______________________________

My favorite meal is_______________________________

Things I do for fun_______________________________

I handle stress by________________________________

I'm scared of____________________________________

General

Hello
Bye
I love you
I miss you
Nice to meet you
Talk to me
Quiet
Kiss
Hugs
Hold hands
My turn
Yor turn
More
All done
Ready
Come

General

YES
Yes
NO
No
Please
Thank you
Good
Bad
Up
Down
Fast
Slow
STOP
Stop
GO
Go
In
Out
I like
I don't like

General

General

I need to leave

I want to go home

I need money

I have an appointment

Can I pay with cash / card?

Wait

Where is the restroom?

I don't feel safe

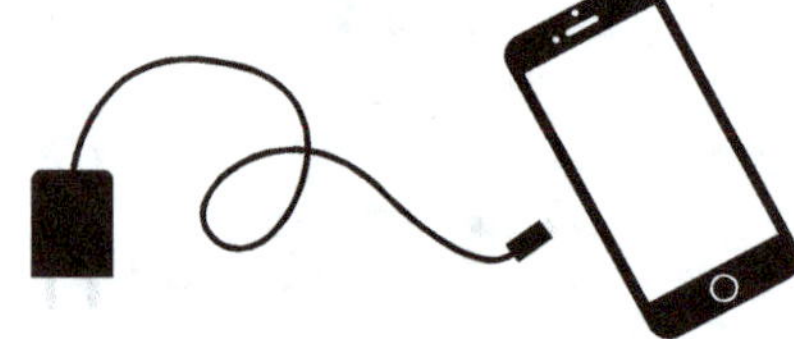

Do you have a phone / charger?

How are you doing?

I'm...

How are you feeling?

I feel...

happy

excited

silly

proud

dreamy

shy

calm

loved

I feel...

bored

sad

scared

angry

stressed

tired

embarrassed

confused

I feel...

hot

cold

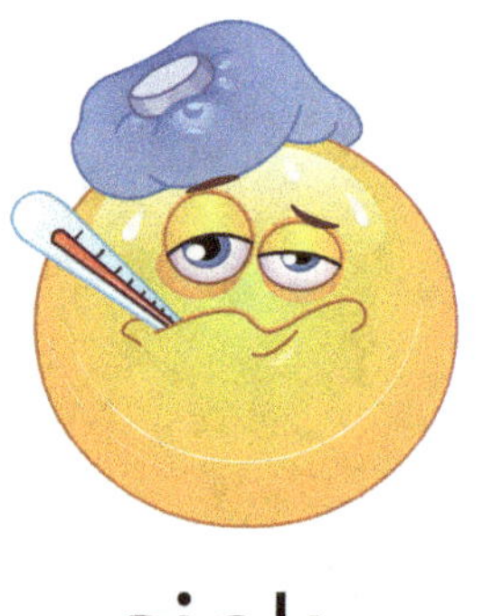

sick

dizzy

hurt

thirsty

hungry

pain

Pain Level

Where is your pain located?

Pain Location

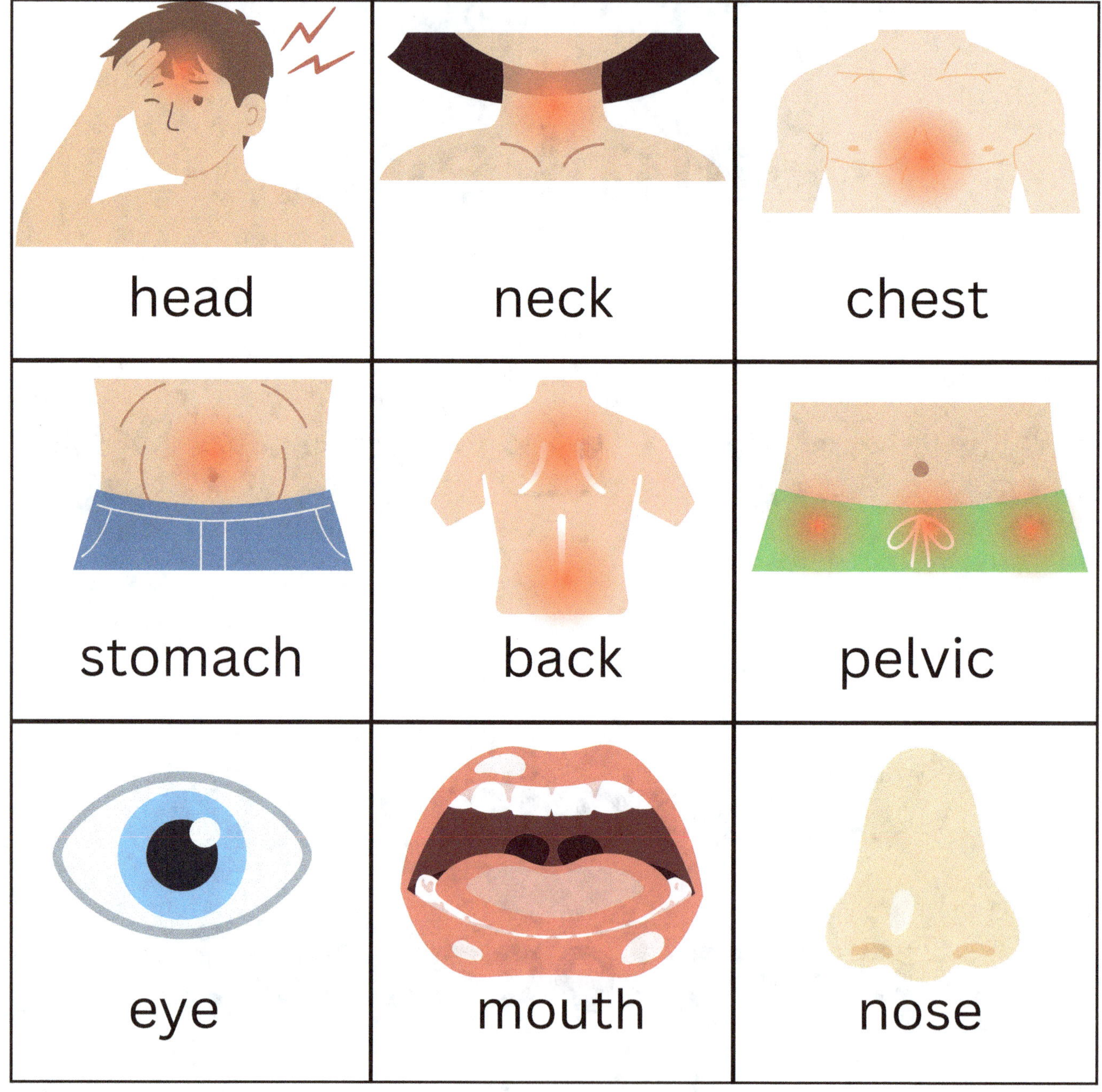

Pain Location

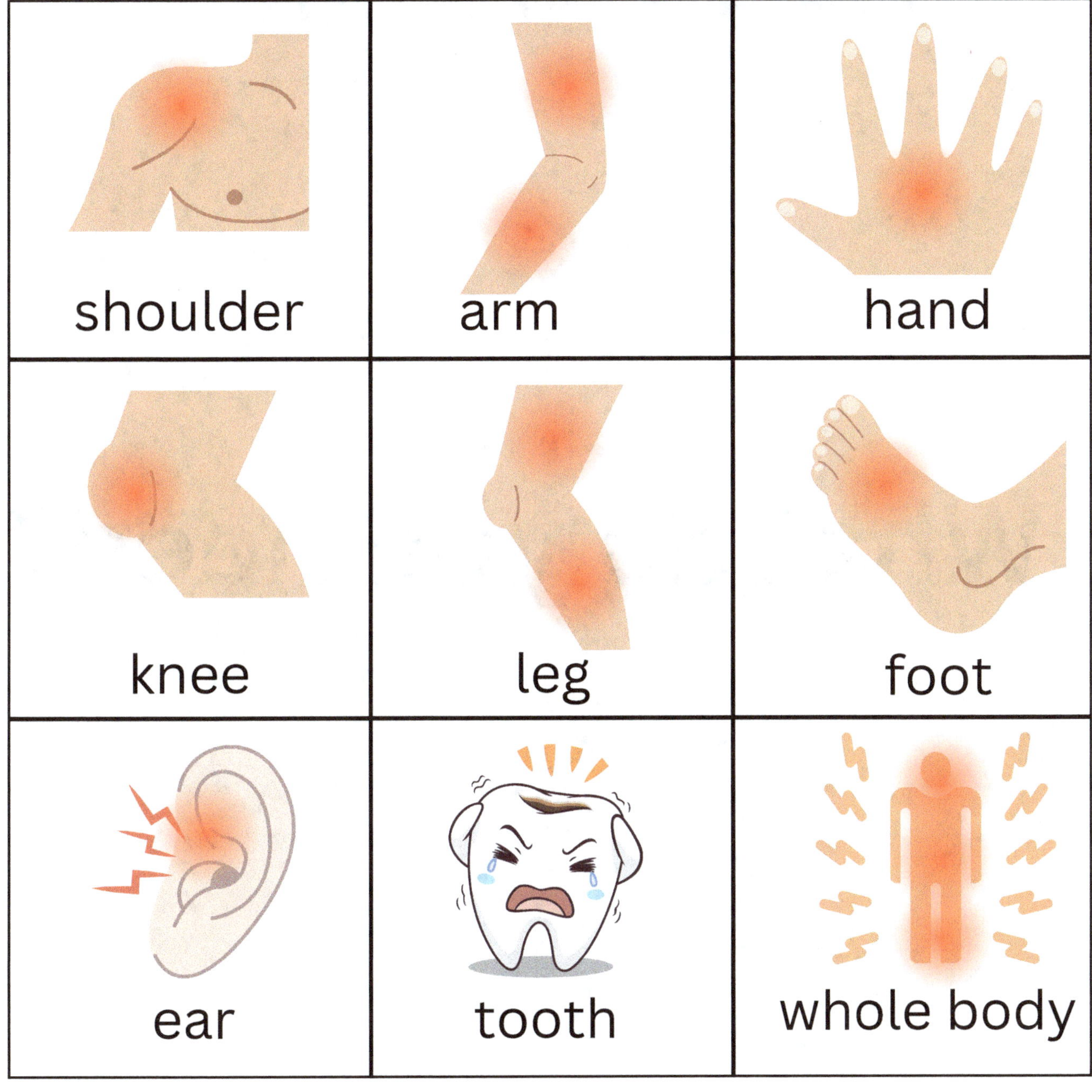

What do you need?

I need...

water

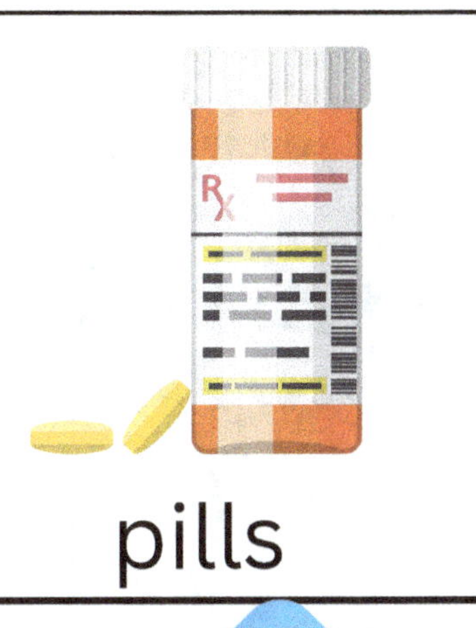

pills

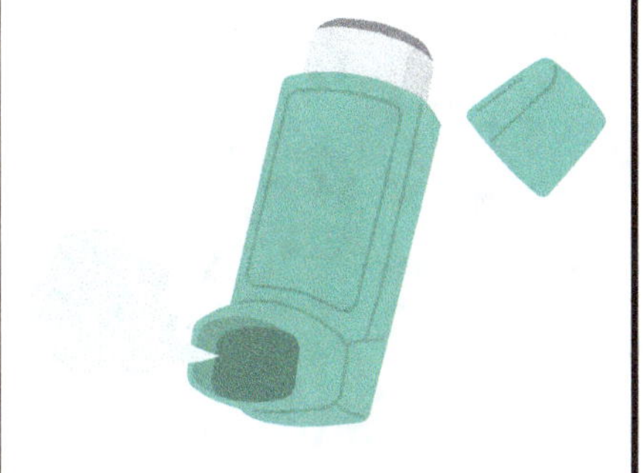

inhaler

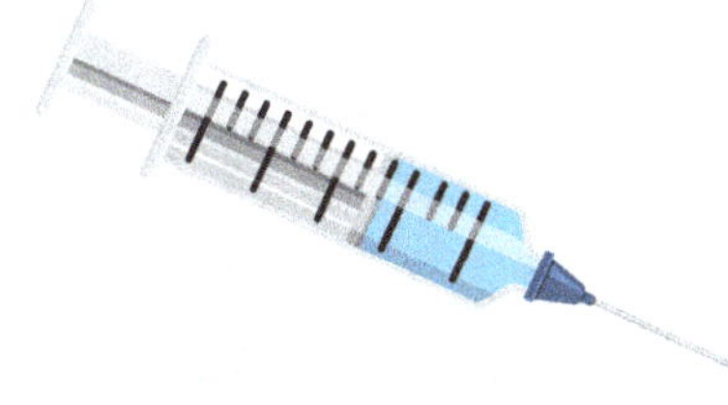

injection

drops

call 911

go to the hospital

call my doctor

I need...

<table>
<tr>
<td>I need...</td>
<td>check temperature</td>
<td>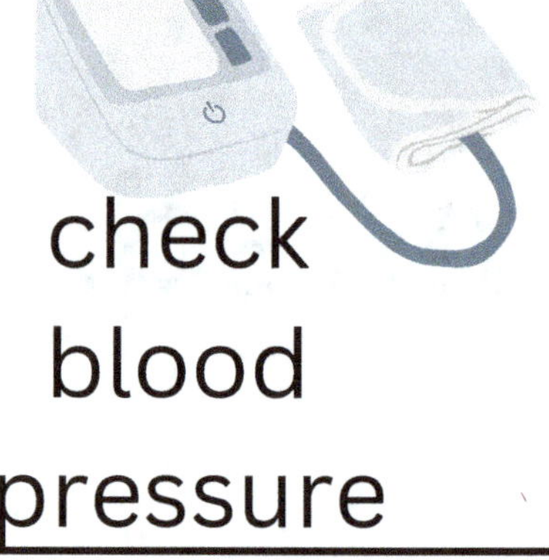check blood pressure</td>
</tr>
<tr>
<td>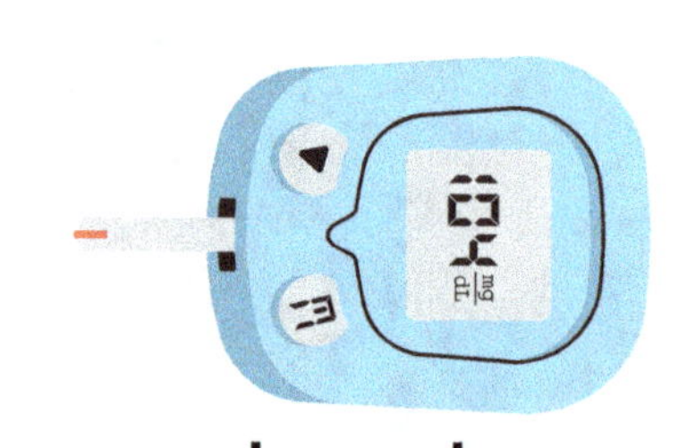check blood sugar</td>
<td>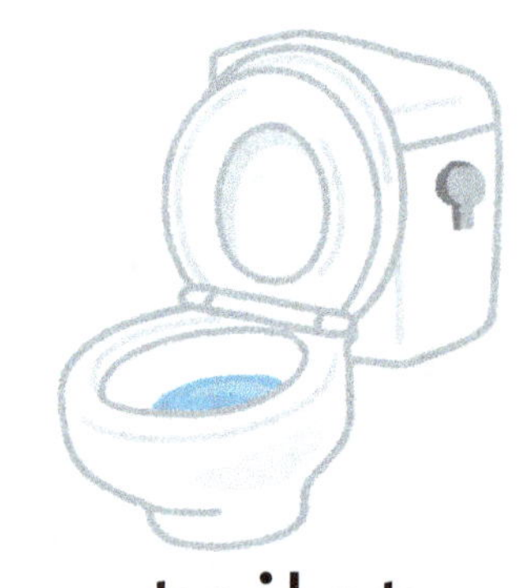toilet</td>
<td>shower</td>
</tr>
<tr>
<td>brush teeth</td>
<td>a bath</td>
<td>wash hands</td>
</tr>
</table>

I need...

help

sit down

stand up

lay down

to walk

to change

glasses

to eat

breakfast

lunch

dinner

snacks

Clothing

dress
shirt
pants
socks
shoes
underwear
pajamas
jacket
hat

Hygiene

pads
toothpaste
toothbrush
soap
lotion
hairbrush
shampoo
conditioner
deodorant
perfume
lip balm

what do you want?

I want...

cold drink

hot drink

milk

fruits

juice

chips

candy

cookies

I want...

 mother	 father
 brother/ sister	 grandma	 grandpa
 laptop	 tablet	 phone

I want...

 board games	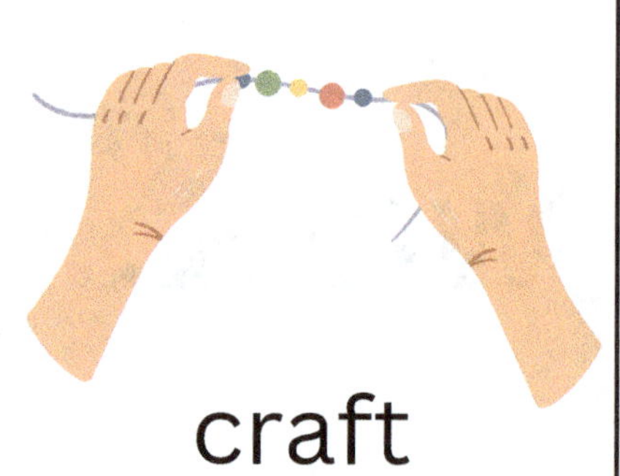 craft	
 video games	 light on / light off	 go for a walk
 to watch tv	 reading book	 to color

Location

Where?

Transportation

Places

church

school

home

store

restaurant

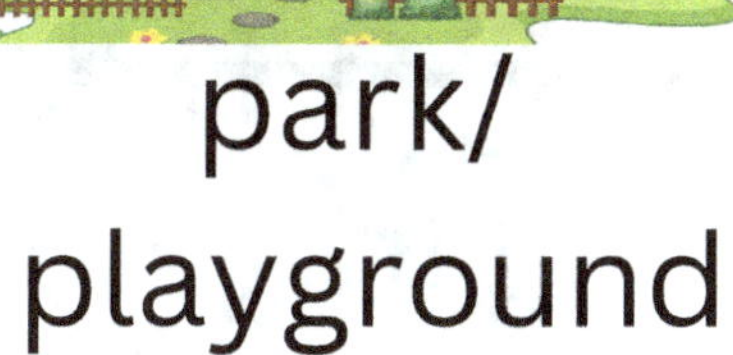

park/
playground

pool/beach

airport

My home

living room

dinning room

bedroom

bathroom

kitchen

backyard

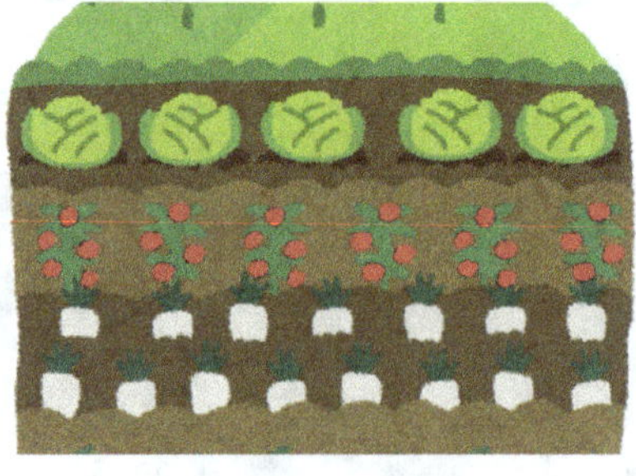

garden

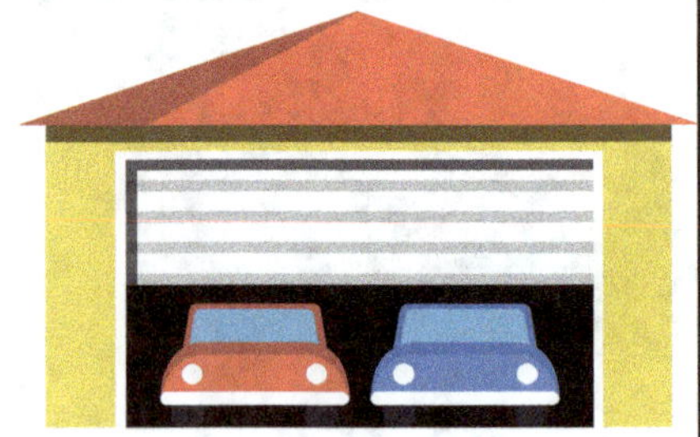

garage

Holidays

Happy
New Year

MERRY
Christmas

Happy
Thanksgiving

HAPPY
HALLOWEEN

HAPPY
BIRTHDAY

Holidays

Happy
Valentine's
Day

HAPPY
EASTER

ST. PATRICK'S DAY

HAPPY
INDEPENDENCE
DAY

Colors

yellow
red
blue
green
purple
pink
orange
black
brown
white
grey

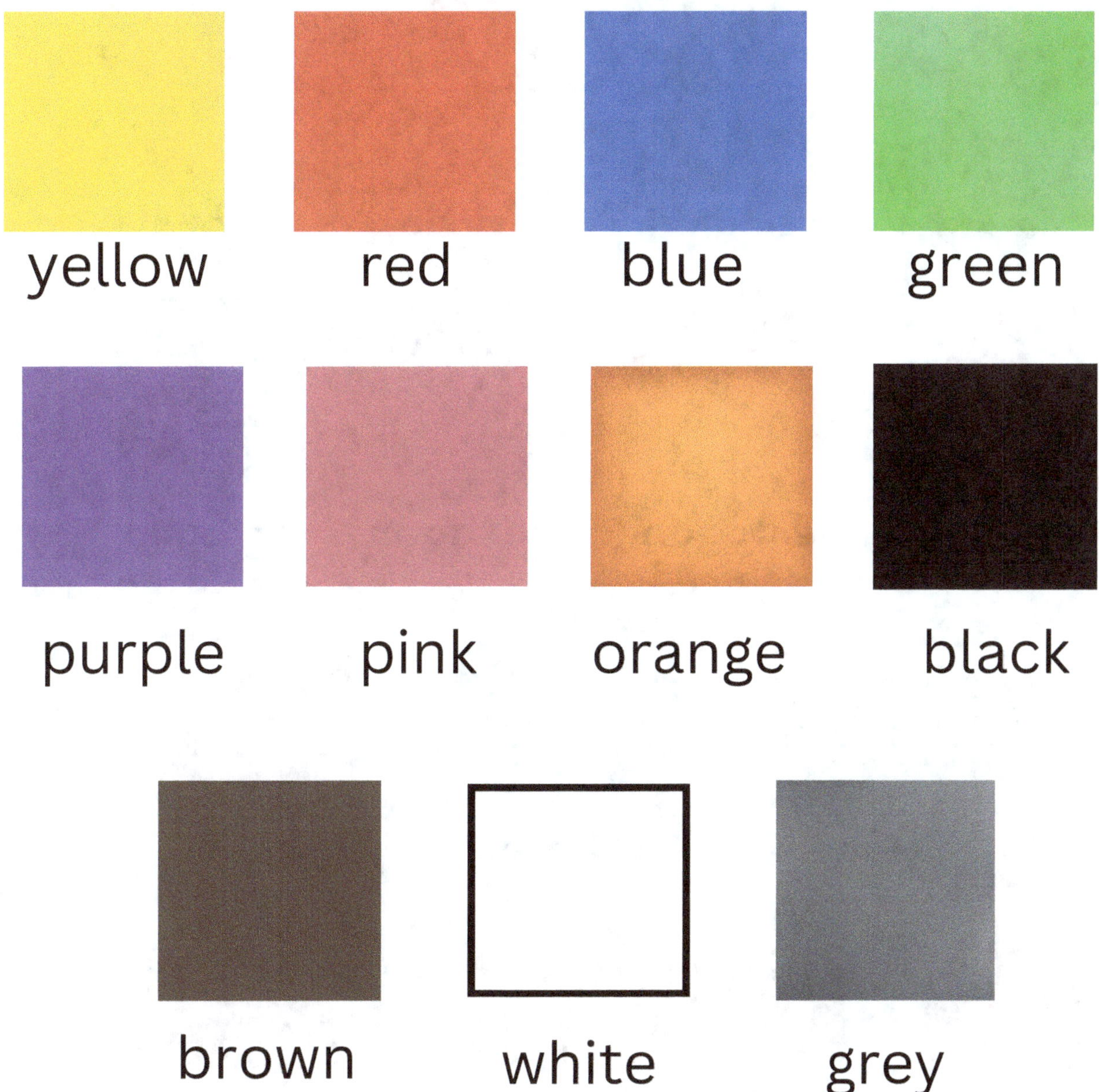

Shapes

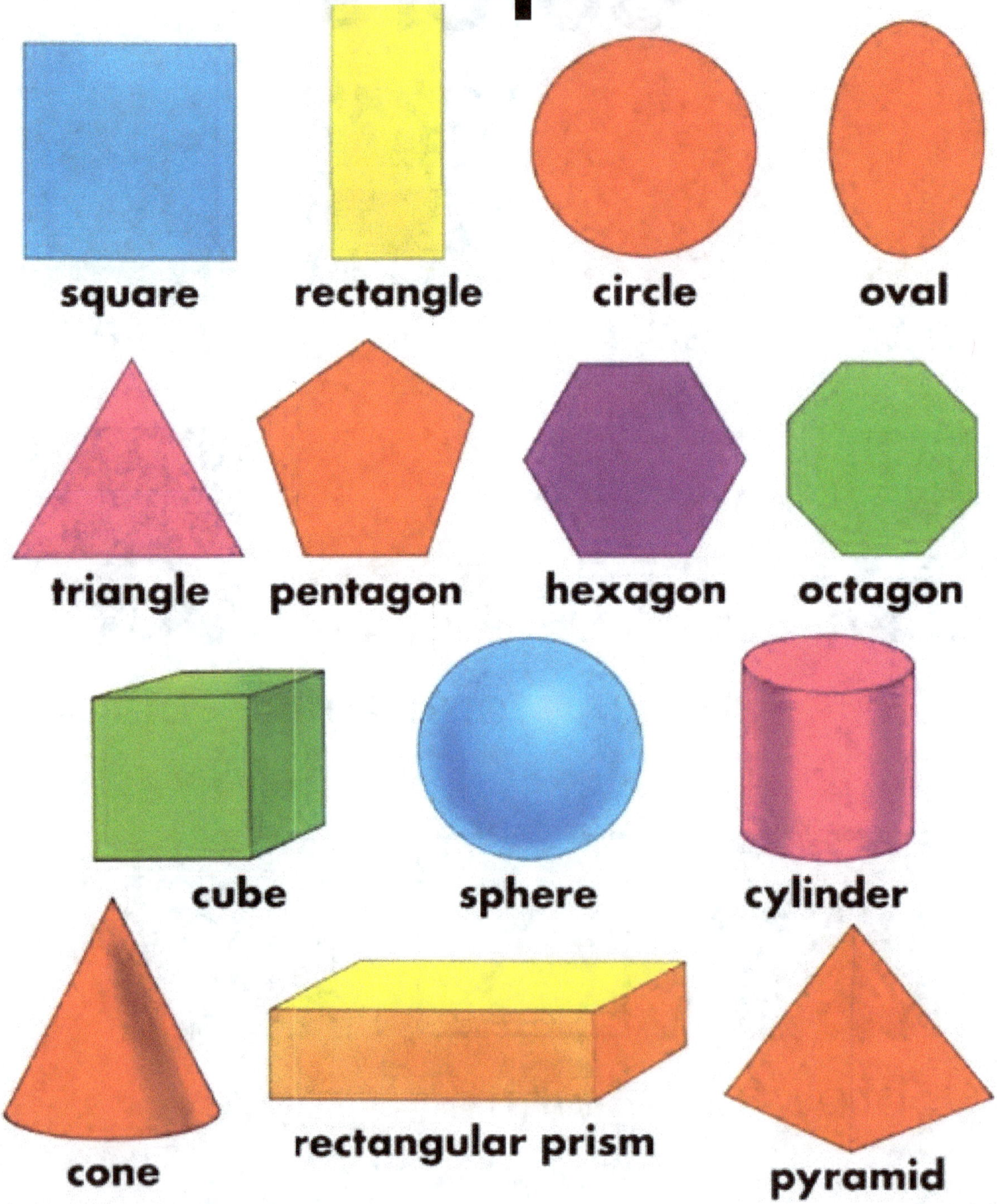

square

rectangle

circle

oval

triangle

pentagon

hexagon

octagon

cube

sphere

cylinder

cone

rectangular prism

pyramid

Calendar

Today is

Sunday	January	1	13	25
Monday	February	2	14	26
Tuesday	March	3	15	27
Wednesday	April	4	16	28
Thursday	May	5	17	29
Friday	June	6	18	30
Saturday	July	7	19	31
	August	8	20	
	September	9	21	
	October	10	22	
	November	11	23	
	December	12	24	

A B C D E F G H I J K
L M N O P Q R S T U V
W X Y Z

a b c d e f g h i j k l
m n o p q r s t
u v w x y z

0 1 2 3 4 5
6 7 8 9 10

Notes